Sit & Solve

LATERAL
THINKING
PUZZLES

**PAUL SLOANE
& DES MacHALE**

Sterling Publishing Co., Inc.
New York

Edited by Claire Bazinet

3 5 7 9 10 8 6 4

Published by Sterling Publishing Co., Inc.
387 Park Avenue South, New York, NY 10016
© 2003 by Paul Sloane & Des MacHale
Distributed in Canada by Sterling Publishing
⁰⁄₀ Canadian Manda Group, One Atlantic Avenue, Suite 105
Toronto, Ontario, Canada M6K 3E7
Distributed in Great Britain by Chrysalis Books
64 Brewery Road, London N7 9NT, England
Distributed in Australia by Capricorn Link (Australia) Pty. Ltd.
P.O. Box 704, Windsor, NSW 2756, Australia
Manufactured in China
All rights reserved

Sterling ISBN 0-8069-5705-0

CONTENTS

Puzzles 4

Answers 62

"It's all in how you look at things."

4

ACKNOWLEDGMENTS

We thank all contributors to the lateral puzzles forum (www.lateralpuzzles.com) and the following people: Craig Humphrey for Here Fido, Michael Schnell for Strange Security, Tim Dowd for A Cover Up, Michael Wolf for Fast Flood, Robert Grey for Lethal Dose, and Eliza Stewart for Hat Check.

INTRODUCTION

The most important muscle in your body is your brain. It has enormous power and potential. No computer can match it. But how much exercise does it get? Is it toned and fit or tired and flabby?

The good news is that you can exercise your brain at all sorts of times and in all sorts of places. The next time you must pause—don't just relax and turn your brain off. Challenge it with these puzzles. As you sit and solve you will be giving your brain muscles a vigorous workout. But be warned—some of these puzzles may take more than one sitting. So get in shape, get thinking, and get solving!

—1—
EASY LATERALS
to get you going

Eye See
A woman's sons are all blue-eyed but two, all brown-eyed but two, and all gray-eyed but two. How many sons does she have?

6

Leg Count
What has six legs but walks on only four?

Who's There?
I have a mouth but do not speak,
I have four eyes but do not see,
I have a bed but do not sleep,
Can you tell me who I be?

Answers on page 62.

Time Was

When in the last 200 years was there a year which read the same upside down?

The Joneses

Mr. and Mrs. Jones have their three sons with them. Each son has with him his wife, his sister, and his son. How many people does that make all together?

Scramble

Rearrange the following group of letters to form a single word:

S N E W G A L R D O I

Four Gs

Can you think of an eight-letter word that contains the letter G four times?

Answers on page 62.

7

Sure Thing

You are challenged to play chess simultaneously by two international chess grandmasters. You don't even know the rules of chess. You get two points for a win and one point for a draw. Can you think of a plan that will gain you at least two points?

Boxed Fruit

8

You have three boxes, all sealed. The first is full of oranges, the second full of lemons, and the third full of a mixture of oranges and lemons. All the boxes are incorrectly labeled. You are allowed to pick a piece of fruit from one box only. How can you now tell which box is which?

Short Cut?

It takes 3 days to go from A to B but 4 days to go from B to A. Why?

Answers on pages 62–63.

Numbering!

A house painter paints numbers on all the houses in a new estate from 1 to number 100. How many times does he paint the number 9 in the process?

Always a First Time

It happened on the second day of February in just one year in the 20th century. That was the first time it had happened in over 1,000 years, but now it is commonplace. What was it?

Got a Code?

a) What does this mean? YYUR YYUB ICUR YY4ME

b) What does this mean? If the **B** mt put :

If the **B** . putting :

Answers on pages 63–64.

9

WALLY QUESTIONS

or kick yourself 101

> Warning: These are trick questions. No lateral puzzle book is complete without some of these examples of sideways thinking.

10

1. What do you get if you cross a brook and a stream?

2. If you have an important letter to write, is it better to write it on an empty stomach or a full stomach?

3. If men have two hands and monkeys have four hands, then what has just three hands?

Answers on page 64.

4. What do reindeer have that no other animals have?

5. Can you spell hard water using just three letters?

6. What kind of butter can you get milk from?

7. What kind of book can a writer never finish?

8. What can stand upright and lie on its face at the same time?

9. What has eight wheels but can carry only one passenger?

10. What do people in Scotland call a little white cat?

11. What kind of tree does a cat hide under during a rainstorm?

12. Where do bats go in the winter?

13. What is made dirty by washing?

Answers on pages 64–65.

—3—

HI-SCI BENT

or science appliance

Meteor, Right?

12

The moon is about a quarter of a million miles from Earth. If a large meteor crashed into the moon, how long would it take for the sound of the explosion to reach Earth?

Floater

If you put a cork in a glass of water, the cork will float to one side. How can you get the cork to float in the middle of the water? (Note: The glass must be sitting on a flat surface. Whirling the glass of water around is not the answer.)

Answers on page 65.

Buck Up

A man is holding a bucket full of water.
He turns the bucket upside down but the bucket
remains full of water. How come? (Before you respond:
the bucket has no lid, the water is not frozen, the man is not in
a space capsule, and he is not swinging the bucket around so that
centrifugal force keeps the water in the bucket.)

Pot Pourri?

A woman has come upon a pot with a mixture of sand, salt,
sawdust, and iron filings in it. How does she manage to separate
the individual substances in the mixture?

Make Way

What can pass through water without getting wet?

Answers on page 65.

Ballooning

You have a helium-filled balloon (lighter than air) in your car and all the windows closed. As you turn a corner, which way does the helium balloon move?

Hole Story

You have a ring made of metal which you heat so that it expands. Does the hole in the middle of the ring get bigger, smaller, or stay the same?

14

Lock Up or Down?

There is a barge in a canal lock. The owner throws an iron anchor off his barge and into the lock. What happens to the water level in the lock—does it go up, down, or stay the same?

Answers on page 66.

Stopper
Starter

You have an antique glass decanter with a glass stopper. The stopper is stuck fast in the neck of the decanter. You have tried pouring hot water over it, but that did not work. What can you do to release the stopper?

No Yoke!

Approximately how many cells are there in an egg yolk?

Close Orbit

The planet nearest the sun is Mercury, then Venus, Earth, Mars, Jupiter, Saturn, Uranus, Neptune, and Pluto. Neptune and Pluto are the farthest from the sun. On average, which planet do you think is closest to Pluto?

Answers on pages 66–67.

—4—
STRANGE DOINGS
what's going on?

Fast Work

Police are called to a murder scene and immediately arrest the caller. Why?

16

Stealth Weapon?

A woman murders her spouse and doesn't leave the house. The police arrive two hours later but can't find the murder weapon. Why not?

Understandable

During WWII, why did the Allies bomb a tiny Polish village with no strategic or military importance?

Answers on pages 67–68.

Flip Flap

An envelope is addressed with the gummed flap closer to the reader's left instead of to the right. Just because of that, a man dies. How come?

W.W.C.!

Winston Churchill, British statesman and former prime minister of England, was once found in the Ladies Rest Room at an important social function. He was not at all embarrassed about being there. Why was that?

Bingo

A man hears a woman calling out a number, and he immediately dies. What was the number?

Answers on page 68.

Au Naturel?

Hundreds of workers are busy in a small confectionery manufacturing plant on a very hot day. There's no air conditioning. How do they keep cool?

And Don't Come Back!

A woman phoned the railway station and asked the price of a ticket to a certain place. How did the clerk immediately know that she wanted a single ticket and not a return ticket?

Eating Disorder

A man was accused of entering a supermarket, opening a package on the shelves and eating a portion of the contents, and walking out without paying anything. What did he plead in his defense?

Answers on page 69.

Firebug

A man buys an expensive carpet and immediately incinerates it. Why?

Speed Lotto

A man spends most of his time trying to find faster and better numbers. What is his job?

Tentative

An explorer is in a tent. It offers no protection from the weather. However, if he leaves it he will die. Why?

Ouch!

What living creature is sometimes one thousand times more valuable when injured than in full health?

Answers on page 69.

SIDELONG VISION

take a second look

Quick Change

Make the triangle at right point downward by moving the very minimum number of balls:

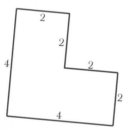

Shape Shift

How can you divide the shape at left into four pieces of equal size and shape?

Answers on page 70.

Match Try

Using just six matches, can you form four equilateral triangles?

2 by 2

a) A 7 by 7 square has two adjacent 1 by 1 squares removed. Can the figure be tiled by 2 by 1 tiles?

b) A 6 by 6 square has two 1 by 1 squares removed from opposite corners. Can this figure be tiled by 2 by 1 tiles?

a)

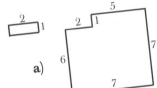

b)

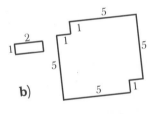

21

Answers on pages 70–71.

Tote These Boxes

a) Place the numbers
1, 2, 3, 4, 5, 6, 7, 8, 9, one
in each box, so that all rows,
columns, and both diagonals
add up to different totals.

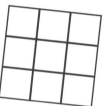

b) Here, place the numbers 1, 2, 3, 4 one in
each box so that all rows, columns, and both
diagonals add up to different totals.

End Up

Move just two matchsticks to make
this dog face to the right instead
of to the left. But, his tail
must stay up!

Answers on page 71.

Dot's Nice

a) Start at any of the nine dots and draw four straight lines so that you go through all nine dots. You must not lift your pen from the paper.

b) How can you draw this circle and the dot at the center without lifting your pen from the paper once you have started?

Licked?

A bottle is partially filled with a liquid, as shown. You have only a ruler. How can you accurately estimate the volume of the bottle?

Answers on pages 71–72.

Sum Matches

How can you place two matches on this clock face in order to divide it into three sections so that the sum of the numbers in each section is the same?

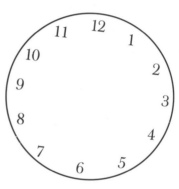

24

Pencil Pals

How can you position six pencils so that every pencil touches each of the other five pencils?

Answers on page 72.

MORE WALLY QUESTIONS

the kicking continues

1. How can you make a positive whole number using just two zeros?

2. What number is always found in the middle of the telephone directory?

3. Chuck took his girlfriend to a restaurant. The cheapest item on the menu was GESG so he ordered it for them both. What did they get?

4. A boy finds a piece of paper with 819 ON written on it. What does it mean?

5. A woman has five children. Half of them are boys— how come?

Answers on page 73.

25

6. What property do the numbers 1, 2, 6, and 10 all have that no other whole number has?

7. What is open when it is shut and shut when it is open?

8. Where can you find a triangle with three right angles?

9. What is it that even the strongest man on earth can hold for only a couple of minutes?

10. Two men got lost while exploring in the desert. Each had a compass. One headed due East and the other headed due West. Two hours later they met. How come?

11. If it takes a clock 2 seconds to strike 2 o'clock, how long will it take to strike 4 o'clock?

12. Bill bets that he can stay under water for 10 minutes without any special breathing equipment. How does he do it?

Answers on pages 73–74.

13. Tom has three, Dick has three, and Harry has three. How many do they have altogether?

14. You have some black socks, blue socks, green socks and grey socks in your drawer. There are twice as many black socks as blue socks and three times as many black socks as green socks. There are twice as many grey socks as green socks. In the dark, how many socks do you need to pull out of the drawer to be sure of getting a pair of matching socks?

15. Tom was born in 1961, the most recent year that is the same turned upside down. How old will Tom be the next time this happens?

27

Answers on page 74.

STORY PUZZLES

leading you in

This type of puzzle is usually enjoyed in a group: a person who knows the answer responds to questions with a "yes" or "no" until the desired solution is deduced. Since that interactivity may not be likely here, hints/clues are provided to nudge you laterally toward our expected correct response.

Glass Phobia?

Why did a woman smash all the light bulbs in her home?

Hints on page 58.
Answer on page 74.

28

Tin Man?

A man puts his unprotected hand into a can of boiling water but does not get burned. Why?

Hanging Button

A man is shown a button suspended by a string inside a corked bottle. It is hanging securely from the cork partway down the bottle. How does he manage to cause the button to drop to the bottom of the bottle without moving the cork in or out of the bottle or without breaking the bottle?

Reversible

A woman bought an expensive piece of equipment and used it very successfully, but for the exact opposite function for which it was intended. What was it?

Hints on page 58.
Answers on page 75.

News to Suit

A commercial company bought dozens of suitcases, filled them with rolled-up newspapers, and never opened them again. Why?

Seeing Green

Why did a man ask to borrow his grumpy neighbor's lawnmower when he really had no intention of cutting his grass?

30

No, Thanks!

A man bought something expensive. He then went out and gave it to a series of total strangers who, in turn, each handed it back to him. What was it?

Hints on page 59.
Answers on pages 75–76.

Be Prepared

A woman wearing a white coat walked down a road. In a pocket she carried a piece of jewelry, a writing implement, and some fuel. Where was she going?

Here, Fido

A man staying at a friend's house made a telephone call. Then he frantically ran around the house looking for the dog. Why?

31

Big Sale?

My wife bought me something I use every day at home or while on vacation, but never when I'm on a business trip. What is it?

Hints on pages 59–60.
Answers on pages 76–77.

Eye See

Everyone was on a first name basis until someone suddenly got something in his eye. What happened?…and when?

Strange Security

A couple feared for the safety of their child, so they went out and bought four glasses and a bottle of vodka. Why?

32

A Cover-Up

A man got rid of something he'd had for a long time. It was only then that he discovered something he hadn't realized was there. And he didn't like it one bit! What was it?

Hints on pages 60–61.
Answers on pages 77–78.

Fast Flood

A man was surprised by a flood, or he would have discovered the murderer. What happened?

Step On It

A man drew some money from a cash machine and hid it in his shoe for safekeeping. He was seen doing it and those who saw followed him and beat him up. However, they didn't take the money. What was that all about?

Fast Trip

Car trips almost always take longer in bad weather than in good weather. In some places in some instances, trips can be much shorter in bad weather than in good. How can this be?

Hints on page 61.
Answers on page 78.

33

MAKE MINE MATH

count on it

Matches

a) Move just one match to correct this equation:

$$VI = II$$

b) Do it differently, adjusting just one match to correct this equation:

$$VI = II$$

c) Now move just one match to correct this equation:

$$II = XXIIII / VIIII$$

Answers on page 79.

34

Pen Tell

Make the following equations correct by adding just one stroke from your pen:

a) $4 + 4 + 4 + 44 = 492$

b) $10\ 10\ 10 = 9.50$

Another Kind of Match

Forty-seven people enter a knockout tennis tournament. How many matches must be played in order to decide the winner?

Digitizer

Using each of the digits 1, 2, 3, 4, 5, 6, 7, 8, 9 once and only once, form two whole numbers one of which is double the other (e.g., numbers 23 and 46, but of course this is not the solution).

Answers on page 79.

Po-table

A farmer sells ten tons of potatoes every year and also grows seed for next year's planting. If his yield is exactly twenty times the amount he plants, what is the least he should plant to ensure a perpetual supply?

Yes–Win Solution

36

A and B play a game as follows: A picks a whole number from 1 to 10 (e.g., 1, 2, 3, etc.). In turn, B adds one number from 1 to 10 to A's number. They play alternately, adding numbers in this way. The first person to reach exactly 100 is the winner. Devise a winning strategy for this game—then try it out on family or friends.

Whole Lot of Shakin'

Is the number of people in the world who have shaken hands with an odd number of people odd or even?

Answers on pages 79–81.

On Tap

It takes 3 minutes for a bath to fill with both taps full on and the plug in. It takes 5 minutes for the bath to empty with the taps off and the plug out. How long will it take for the bath to fill with both taps on and the plug out?

No Dart About It

Each dart in a match scores 16, 17, 23, 24, 39, or 40 points. How many darts must be thrown to make a score of exactly 100?

37

Eight Ball

How many different ways can you make up 1000, using exactly eight eights and no other numbers and the usual mathematical operations of arithmetic?

Answers on page 81.

VISUAL PUZZLES

hard on the eyes

Smart Kid

A boy's telephone number is 741-5963. He is able to remember it by thinking of just one letter. Which letter?

Working the Angles

The outer and inner triangles are both equilateral and the circle touches all three sides of the outer triangle. If the area of the inner triangle is 10 square centimeters, what is the area of the outer triangle?

10

Answers on page 82.

Baaa

A farmer has 13 fencing panels of equal size which form six sheep pens of equal size and shape as shown. When one of the panels is stolen, how does he make six pens of equal size and shape using the remaining 12 panels?

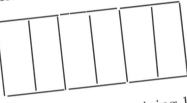

The P Place

An engineer wishes to build a pump house (P) by a river in order to pump water to towns A and B. Where should P be placed so that the length of the pipe AP + BP is as short as possible?

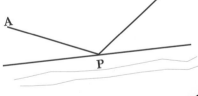

Answers on page 83.

Trapple!

A farmer wishes to plant 7 apple trees—in six rows with exactly three trees in each row! How does he do it?

Dunkin' or Krispy?

(40)

The length of the tangent, as shown, from the outer circle to the inner circle is 5 cm. What is the area of the doughnut (annulus) shape?

5 cm

Don't Be Lax

In this diagram, OA = 4 and AB = 3. What is the length of AX?

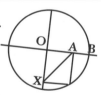

Answers on pages 84–85.

Hat Trick

A, B, C, and D have hats on. They know the hats are either black or white and are not all the same color, but can't see the color of their own. A sees none, B sees A's hat, C sees A and B's, D sees A, B, and C's. Who suddenly announces that he knows what color hat he is wearing?

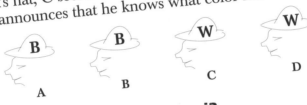

A   B   C   D

41

Missouri?

How can you measure the width of a wide river you cannot cross if all you have is a single yardstick?

Answers on page 85.

Eye Test

Here are a front and an overhead view
of an object. What does it look like?

Passing Grade in Art

A pair of compasses can be used to draw a
perfect circle. How can the same pair of
compasses be used to draw a perfect
ellipse? You must keep the compasses in the same position,
not alter their radius
during drawing.

Answers on page 86.

42

—10—
UNCOMMON LATERALS

side saddle

Three-peat!

a) How many letters are there in the correct answer to this question? (First solution)

b) How many letters are there in the correct answer to this question? (Second solution)

c) How many letters are there in the correct answer to this question? (Third solution)

43

Postpaid

A man with two hobbies took great care to send a letter to an address which he knew did not exist. Why?

Answers on pages 86–87.

Too Long!

A man has a fishing rod thirteen feet long which he wishes to mail, but Post Office regulations stipulate that no parcel can be longer than twelve feet. The fishing rod is all one piece and he cannot shorten it; what does he do?

InDEFinite

44

The word "inDEFinite" contains three consecutive letters of the alphabet consecutively. Can you find a word which contains four consecutive letters of the alphabet consecutively?

Poker Face

A boy and a girl are playing poker. The girl has a royal flush and the boy has four aces. Who wins the game?

Answers on page 87.

Button Up

You have 9 buttons and 4 cups. How can you put an odd number of buttons into each cup using all the buttons and all the cups?

Somehow

From what can you take away the whole and still have some left?

How Irregular!

How can you make a raw egg float exactly half way up in a glass of water?

Nonplussed

Can you see what is remarkable about the equation: One plus twelve = Two plus eleven?

Answers on pages 87–88.

Evening the Odds

It is known that a certain coin is faulty. When it is tossed it lands heads much more often that it lands tails. How can two people toss it to make a fair 50/50 bet?

Elbow Room

How would you arrange five circular coins so that each coin touches all of the other four coins?

46

Black Sheep?

Chuck's family are all U.S. citizens and they always vote Republican. At the last election, Chuck voted Republican but his uncle did not vote Republican. Why?

Answers on page 88.

—11—

LOGIC PUZZLES

laterally speaking

A-stounding!

What is the smallest positive whole number which contains the letter "a" when written out in words?

Check This Out

Four checkers are placed in a line as follows: WW__BB. Can you swap the positions of the checkers to BB__WW using the following rules? The checkers can either move one space to the side, or jump over an opponent's checker to an empty space. White checks can move only to the right, and black checkers can move only to the left.

Answers on page 89.

Cube It
A cube is cut into 27 identical smaller cubes using six plane cuts. Can the same objective be achieved with fewer cuts, perhaps by rearranging the pieces after each cut?

Don't Tell
A woman is less than a hundred years old. When her age is divided by seven the remainder is two; when her age is divided by five the remainder is four, and when her age is divided by three, the remainder is two. What is her age?

Time Out
A holy man sets out to climb a mountain up the only path at midday on Tuesday. He reaches the summit at midnight, prays, fasts and then sleeps until midday on Wednesday. At midday he starts

Answers on page 89.

down the mountain
path very slowly and carefully and
reaches the bottom of the mountain at midnight.
Can you show that there must be some time on the
clock such that he was at the same point on the path going
up on Tuesday and coming down on Wednesday at that time?

Wrap Rap

To promote sales of its new product, the CHOCKOBLOCK candy
bar, a company gives away a free bar in exchange for every
ten wrappers of CHOCKOBLOCK bars a kid hands over to the
shopkeeper. What fraction of a CHOCKOBLOCK bar is a
CHOCKOBLOCK wrapper worth?

Bad Bill

A man sees a pair of boots in a shoe shop window
priced $30. He goes in and buys them

Answers on page 90.

with a $50 bill but
the shopkeeper has no change so he
goes next door and swaps the $50 bill for five
$10 bills. He gives $20 to the customer who departs
with the boots. A few minutes later the person next door
rushes in screaming that the $50 bill he was given is a forgery
so the shopkeeper has to give him a fresh $50 bill from the till.
The question is, how much did the shopkeeper lose on the
transaction, counting the boots as worth $30?

50

Lethal Dose

Once upon a time, there was a king, and in his kingdom poisons
worked differently from how they work here. There, if you
have taken poison, then the only cure is to take a stronger
poison afterwards. If you do, then neither poison has
any adverse effect, whilst if by mistake you take a
weaker poison, both poisons have their full

Answers on page 90–91.

(and lethal) effect.

In order to thin out the ranks of the poisoners in the kingdom, the king decided to hold a contest to determine the best poisoner in all the land. Once all the entries were in, the rules were explained. In each round, the alchemists would be paired off, and each of them would provide a flask of poison. Each would then drink from their opponent's flask, and then from their own. The one who survived would go through to the next round. Any attempt to withdraw from the competition would mean instant execution. At length, the competitors were reduced to a single pair. One of them, the night before the contest, managed to get hold of a tiny sample of his opponent's poison, and to his horror realized that it was far stronger than anything he had or could hope to produce. Then he realized that there was a way he could win the contest after all. How did he do it?

Answers on page 91.

Duel à Trois

Three men, Alf, Bert, and Con, decide to fight an unusual duel. They will stand at the corners of an equilateral triangle and take it in turns to shoot. When it is a man's turn he can take one shot at whomever he wants. They will keep taking turns until only one man survives. Now it is known that Alf is the best shot and hits his target 90% of the time, Bert is the second best and hits 75% of the time. Con hits his target only 50% of the time. Lots are drawn and it is decided that Con will shoot first and Bert second (if he has survived). Who should Con aim at and who has the best chance of winning?

52

Hat Check

A group of 20 men have been sentenced to death. They are told that the next morning they will be taken out, lined up so that they see everyone in front

Answers on page 91–92.

of them but no-one behind them, and buried in sand so they cannot look around. They will each have a hat put on their head. Each hat is either white or black. Then, starting with the man at the back (who can see all 19 hats in front of him) they are each in turn required to guess the color of their hat. They can each say one word–either "black" or "white." If they correctly guess the color of their hat they go free. If not they are executed. They are then left to discuss this between themselves until morning. What strategy should they adopt to save the largest number and how many can they be sure of saving?

Early Pickup

A man returned from work every day by train, arriving at the station at exactly 7:30 pm. His wife drove to meet him at the station and she took him home in the car. She always drove at a steady 20 mph

Answers on page 92–93.

and they always
arrived home at the same time each
day. One day he caught an earlier train but did
not get a chance to tell his wife, so he started to walk
home at a steady 3 mph. His wife set out at her usual time
and saw him as she was driving to the station. She picked him up
and returned home. They reached home 20 minutes earlier than
normal. At what time did she pick him up?

54

Crossings

Four people have to cross a narrow bridge in the dark. They
have one torch between them which must be used on the crossings.
One or two can cross at a time but not more than two. One of
them can cross in 1 minute, one in 2 minutes, one in 4 minutes
and one in 10 minutes. What is the shortest elapsed time for
them all to cross the bridge?

Answers on page 93.

Clock on a String

You have two strings which will burn for one hour each but they burn in an unpredictable way so that you cannot be sure that half the string would burn, say, in half an hour. Using the strings, how can you time exactly 45 minutes?

Secret Numbers

Three logical people are given a piece of paper, each with a different number on it. Each person knows only his own number. They are told that the sum of two of the three numbers is 25 and the product of two of the numbers is 120. They are then asked to guess the three numbers. None can do so. They are asked a second time to guess the three numbers. Again they cannot do so. They are asked a third time and now they all state the correct three numbers. What are they?

Answers on page 93–95.

—12—
YET MORE
WALLIES
final kicks

56

1. What comes after e in the alphabet?
2. What is the hardest thing about learning to ride a bicycle?
3. When did England begin with an E and end with an E?
4. What comes with a motorbike, is not needed by the motorbike, but the motorbike can't go without it?
5. The more you take away the bigger it gets; the more you add the smaller it becomes. What is it?

Answers on page 96.

6. What joins two people but touches only one of them?

7. Otto's car is expensive and reliable but for some strange reason it starts badly most Wednesdays. Why might that be?

8. How do you divide 11 potatoes evenly between 4 boys?

9. What has four legs and two arms?

10. There were ten cats in a boat on a lake and one cat jumped out of the boat into the water. How many cats were left in the boat?

11. Why was six afraid?

Answers on page 96.

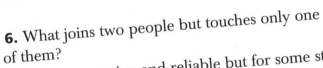

HINTS/CLUES

Glass Phobia?
What do lightbulbs do? This scenario might sound familiar to some moviegoers.

Tin Man?
Is boiling water always burning hot? The man's hand was normal; he was normal–though very fit.

Hanging Button
What could affect the string through the glass?

Reversible
It's much bigger than a bread box, but used for a similar purpose.

Answers on page 74–75.

News to Suit

The newspapers aren't important. What kind of company would have a use for "dummy" suitcases?

Seeing Green

What response is expected from the grumpy neighbor? The man's green lawn brought to mind another more enjoyable activity.

No, Thanks!

The man fully expected the item to be returned to him each time. He was on a trip.

Be Prepared

Certain people often wear white coats. What could the carried items have in common?

Answers on page 75–76.

Here, Fido

Who/where could he have called? What purpose could finding his friend's dog serve? He wanted information.

Big Sale?

The fact that the wife bought the item is a big hint. She is there when he uses it—and she insists upon it!

60

Eye See

A great many people were affected—and continue to be. It's in the history books.

Strange Security

Why four glasses, not two? It didn't have to be vodka. Alcohol can be deadly.

Answers on page 76–77.

A Cover-Up

He couldn't see it before, now he really had to face up to it. No, he couldn't just put back what he got rid of.

Fast Flood

The flooding was not unexpected, but he was in a relaxed state. The man was not a criminal but he did not call the police.

Step On It

It wasn't just random violence, he was attacked for what he did. So, what is different about those banknotes?

Fast Trip

Bad weather needn't be all bad. How does different weather affect roads?

Answers on page 78.

61

ANSWERS

1 —
EASY LATERALS

Eye See
Three.

Leg Count
A rider on horseback.

Who's There?
Why, the river
Mississippi, of course.

Time Was
1881 and 1961. (Did you
get them both?)

The Joneses
There are Mr. and Mrs.
Jones, their three sons, three
daughters-in-law, three grandsons,
and their daughter: 12 in all.

Scramble
A SINGLE WORD.

Four Gs
Giggling (goggling or glugging are
also acceptable).

Sure Thing
If you play black in one game
and white in the other then
you can effectively have
one grandmaster

play the other.
Let one grandmaster make a move and then copy it to the other board. When your second opponent makes his reply, you use that move in the first game, and so on.

Boxed Fruit

Take a piece of fruit from the box labeled "oranges and lemons." That box is incorrectly labeled so it must be either all oranges or all lemons. Say you pick an orange. Then you know this is the box of oranges. The box marked lemons does not contain just lemons and it does not have just oranges so it must be the mixture, and the box marked "oranges and lemons" must have the lemons.

Short Cut?

A is Friday, B is Monday (or similarly spaced days).

Numbering!

20 times: 9, 19, 29, 39, 49, 59, 69, 79, 89, 90, 91, 92, 93, 94, 95, 96, 97, 98, 99. Many people overlook the 90 or the two 9s in 99.

Always a First Time

February second in 2000 (still in the 20th century) is written 2-2-2000. All of the digits used are even. The previous time that happened was the 28th of August, 888!

Got a Code?

a) Too wise you are, too wise you be. I see you are too wise for me.

b) If the grate be (great B) empty put coal on (colon). If the grate be full stop (period) putting coal on.

2— WALLY QUESTIONS

1. Wet feet!
2. It's better to write the letter on paper.
3. An alarm clock.
4. Baby reindeer.
5. ICE.
6. A goat!
7. His or her autobiography.
8. A gravestone.
9. A pair of roller skates.
10. A kitten.
11. A very wet tree.
12. Most baseball

bats go in the garage in the winter.
13. The wash water.

3—HI-SCI BENT

Meteor, Right?
The sound would never reach the Earth as sound cannot travel in a vacuum.

Floater
Carefully add water, filling the glass to the brim. Surface tension will make the top convex and the cork will float to the highest point— the center of the glass.

Buck Up
He is under water.

Pot Pourri?
Use a magnet to remove the iron. Add water to the mixture. This makes the sawdust float to the top to be scooped up. The salt dissolves in the water but the sand does not, so the water can be filtered or poured off, leaving the sand. Finally, the water is boiled off to leave the salt.

Make Way
Light.

Ballooning

The balloon will move opposite to the direction that other objects (and the air in the car) move. So it moves inward on bends, forwards when you accelerate, and backwards when you brake. This is because the air in the car rushes the other way, pushing the lighter balloon.

Hole Story

The ring expands uniformly in all dimensions, so the hole gets bigger.

Lock Up or Down?

The water level in the lock goes down. When it was in the boat, the anchor displaced its own weight of water–it pushed the boat down and the water level up. When the anchor is in the lock, it displaces only its own volume of water which is less, so the barge rises in the lock and the water level goes down.

Stopper Starter

You must heat only the neck to get it to expand. One way is to rub it fast with a cloth or piece of string to generate heat by friction.

No Yoke!

Exactly one.

Close Orbit

Surprisingly, the planet nearest to Pluto *on average* is Mercury. Neptune and Pluto are the two farthest from the Sun but their orbits are not aligned so they are often diametrically opposite on either side of the Sun.

4 — STRANGE DOINGS

Fast Work

The murder took place in a factory at night. The factory contained just the murder victim and the night watchman, who phoned to report the crime. Just before the murder took place there was a heavy snowfall. Since no tracks lead either to or from the factory, the police concluded rightly that the night watchman did it.

Stealth Weapon?

The woman hit her husband on the head with a solidly frozen chicken. She then cooked and ate the "weapon."

Understandable

The Polish village had a 13-letter name, unusual in that it had lots of Zs, Xs, Ks and a J in it. The allied code-breakers were able to see the German transmissions but not decode them. The next day they watched and waited for a German code transmission that included a strange combination of code letters. When they saw it, they were finally able to break the German codes.

Flip Flap

The envelope contained an X-ray transparency. It was taken out of the envelope with left and right reversed, so a healthy lung was removed by mistake and the unfortunate patient died.

W.W.C.!

Winston Churchill was born prematurely in the Ladies Rest Room while his mother attended a ball.

Bingo

The number the man heard was 4 ("Fore!"). The man was hit on the head by a golf ball and killed.

Au Naturel?

The workers flap their wings to keep cool. They are bees making honey.

And Don't Come Back!

The woman asked the price of a ticket for a coffin to be sent to the crematorium.

Eating Disorder

Innocent. He had opened a package of cookies marked "25% extra free" and simply ate only the free ones.

Firebug

The carpet is part of an estate auction from a goldsmith's premises. The buyer incinerates it for the gold dust it most surely contains.

Speed Lotto?

He's an anesthesiologist. He who looks for better anesthetics to make people number.

Tentative

The explorer is sick and in an oxygen tent.

Ouch!

The creature is an oyster, which sometimes produces a pearl when it has been attacked and injured in some way.

Quick Change

Move just 3 balls. The top one straight downward to the bottom center and the end balls just above, left and right, straight up to the new top line.

70

Shift Shape

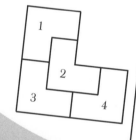

Match Try

Use the third dimension to make a pyramid (a tetrahedron to be precise).

2 by 2

a) No. The figure contains 47 squares (49 − 2) which is odd, so it cannot be filled with tiles of size 2.

b) No. Imagine that the original 6 by 6 square is colored with adjacent squares alternately black and white—like a chessboard. Then both the squares removed are the same color.

So there remain 15 squares of one color and 17 of the other. If the 2 by 1 tiles are half black and half white, then the task is clearly impossible.

Tote These Boxes

a)

1	2	3
8	9	4
7	6	5

This is one solution, but there are many others.

b) You need six different totals, but the minimum is $2 + 1 = 3$ and the maximum is $4 + 3 = 7$. There are only 5 possible totals: 3, 4, 5, 6, 7. So the task is impossible.

End Up

Dot's Nice

a) To solve this noted puzzle you need to think, and move, "outside the box"– which is where the expression comes from.

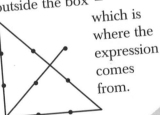

fold the paper as shown to draw the figure.

Licked?

Measure the height of the liquid in the bottle and measure the diameter of the base of the bottle. Then calculate the volume of the liquid (base area by height). Now, turn the bottle upside down and measure the height of the section of air now at the top of the upturned bottle. Calculate

b) You

that volume, then add the two volumes together to get the volume of the entire bottle.

Sum Matches

Place the matchsticks isolating 11, 12, 1, 2 and 10, 3, 9, 4 and 8, 5, 7, 6. Each section sums to 26.

Pencil Pals

Position three pencils with erasers touching each other, then position three more on top as shown.

6 — MORE WALLY QUESTIONS

1. Weld 0 and 0 to make 8.

2. 1. The telephONE directory.

3. Scrambled eggs.

4. It's a raffle ticket (NO 618) held upside down.

5. All of her children are boys, so half are boys also.

6. They all have just three letters.

7. A level crossing (where a railway line crosses a road).

8. On the surface of a sphere.

9. His breath.

10. The two men were not together when they got lost. They had nothing to do with each other until they chanced to meet.

11. It will take the clock six seconds to strike four o'clock. There is one interval between the first and second strike and that is what takes two seconds. There are three intervals between

73

the first and fourth strike so it will take three times as long.

12. Bill holds a glass of water over his head.

13. Three. Tom, Dick and Harry are brothers. Each has three sisters so altogether they have three sisters.

14. You need to take 5 socks to be sure of a pair. If you pull out 4 then you might

have black, blue, green and gray. The proportions of socks in the drawer are irrelevant.

15. Tom will be 4048 as this will not happen again until 6009.

7 — STORY PUZZLES

Glass Phobia?

The woman is blind and is being pursued by a murderer. In the dark, he will be at a disadvantage if he cannot switch on lights. (From the Warner Brothers movie "Wait Until Dark.")

Tin Man?

The man is on a high mountain. Water boils at much lower temperatures at high altitude because of the lower air pressure, so he wasn't burned.

Hanging Button

The man uses a magnifying glass to focus the sun's rays on the string until it burns through. The button then drops.

Reversible

An Eskimo woman bought a refrigerator in order to keep her food from getting too cold.

News to Suit

An airport used suitcases filled with newspapers at a luggage carousel to appease travelers waiting for their suitcases to arrive. The dummy cases made it look as though some luggage was arriving, and this made the passengers less impatient.

Seeing Green

He really wants to borrow his neighbor's golf clubs but knows that if he asks for them

75

the neighbor will say "No, I intend to play golf." So he asks to borrow the lawnmower and when the neighbor says, "No, I plan to mow the lawn today," the man responds, "In that case you won't be needing your golf clubs. Can I borrow them, please?"

76

No, Thanks!

A camera. The man was a tourist visiting many places and asking people to take his photograph in them.

Be Prepared

She was a chemistry teacher on her way to a school's chemistry lab. Prepared to give a lesson on carbon, she had a diamond, a pencil, and a lump of coal to show carbon's different forms.

Here, Fido

The man had phoned an airline to arrange a flight. They said they would call him back and asked for his phone number. He did not know his friend's number but knew it was on the tag on the dog's collar, so he chased the dog to get it.

Big Sale?

My wife bought me a plastic clip that goes on my nose to stop me from snoring. I need it if my wife is with me, but not if I am traveling alone.

Eye See

It happened in 1066. The Saxons in England did not use surnames. They would say John the shepherd or Thomas the butcher. When Saxon king Harold got an arrow in his eye at the battle of Hastings in 1066, William the Conqueror won. The Normans took control of England and made everyone use surnames.

Strange Security

The concerned couple lived in the desert in New Mexico where there are many poisonous scorpions. They made the purchases and put each of the four legs of the baby's crib in a glass containing a little of the alcohol. Scorpions can climb ordinary furniture legs, but they cannot climb glass and they hate alcohol! It's possible to kill a scorpion by pouring alcohol on it.

A Cover-Up

When the man shaved off his beard he found that he had acquired a double chin.

Fast Flood

The man was sitting in a lounge chair on the beach engrossed in a murder mystery. When he put the book down and closed his eyes for a moment, the tide came in and washed the book away. So he never found out who the murderer was.

Step On It!

He was away on holiday and the banknotes he put in his shoe had the King's portrait on them. It was considered a terrible insult to put your foot on a picture of the King, so concerned locals took revenge.

Fast Trip

In places like Northern Finland, many lakes freeze over solidly in winter. In summer, it takes a long time to drive around the lakes, but roads made over the ice in winter make the journey much quicker—even in a snowstorm!

8 — MAKE MINE MATH

Matches

Move one match and…

a) VI = II becomes XI = II

b) VI = II becomes V̄I = I

c) II = XXIII / VII becomes
   π = XXII / VII.
   (Pi is roughly approximated as 22/7.)

Pen Tell I

Add one pen stroke and…

a) 4 + 444 + 44 = 492

b) 10 T0 10 = 9.50

Another Kind of Match

If 47 people enter and one person wins there must be 46 losers. So there must be 46 games in total since each game produces one loser.

Digitizer

The two numbers are 6729 and 13458.

Po-table

The farmer must plant 10/19 of a ton of potatoes. If he plants x tons each year then his yield is 20x tons. He uses 10 tons so what is

left is
$$20x - 10 \text{ tons.}$$
This equals x.
$$20x - 10 = x$$
$$19x = 10$$
$$x = 10/19$$

Yes–Win Solution

If you can reach 89 then whatever your opponent plays next you will be able to get to 100 after him and win. If you can reach 78 then you reach 89. So it goes down in 11s. The key totals to reach are 89, 78, 67, 56, 45, 34, 23, 12. So if you go first you should play

1 and then get to 12 on your second go. If you go second and your opponent plays anything other than 1 then go straight to 12.

Whole Lot of Shakin'

Every handshake is two events— one for each participant. Therefore the total number of handshakes made by everyone will be an even number. Some people will have shaken an even number of hands. If you take those away you are left with an even number. Some people will have shaken hands an odd number of hands. But there must be an even number of them because an even total cannot be made up of an odd number of odd numbers.

On Tap

The bath fills at one third of a bath per minute and empties at one fifth of a bath per minute. So, if both effects take place at the same time, the bath fills at two fifteenths of a bath per minute and would fill in seven and a half minutes.

At least, that is the model answer. In the real world, however, the rate at which the bath empties is not flat. It varies according to the amount of water pressure that is above the outgoing plug hole. So, the "real" answer to the posed question is, very likely, that the tub never fills.

No Dart About It

Six darts: four 17s and two 16s.

Eight Ball

Here are two ways:
$8 + 8 + 8 + 88 + 888 = 1000$,
$(8888 - 888)/8 = 1000$.
Can you find another?

VISUAL PUZZLES

Smart Kid

He simply remembers the letter N, which is the shape formed by his number on the phone keypad. (Many other letters can serve a similar purpose for lateral-thinking phone users.)

Working the Angles

The two triangles are similar. Now for the lateral part–imagine the triangle inside the circle is rotated through 180 degrees. It now forms four triangles of equal size inside the large triangle. So the area of the large triangle must be 40.

82

Baaa

He does
it like so:

Trapple!

He plants the
trees like this:

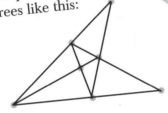

The P Place

Reflect point B in the nearest river
bank to form B', then draw a line
from A to B'. Where this line
crosses the river is the point P.

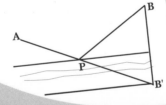

Dunkin' or Krispy?

If the large circle has
radius R and the small circle has
radius r, then the area of the
doughnut is $(\pi R^2 - \pi r^2)$.
Construct a right-angled
triangle from the
center, O, to

either end of the tangent. For this triangle we know that $R^2 = r^2 + 5^2$. So $25 = R^2 - r^2$. Multiplying both sides of the equation by π, the area of the doughnut is therefore 25π cm².

Don't Be Lax

The radius of the circle is OA + AB = 7. OAXY is a rectangle so AX = OY
= the radius
= 7.

Hat Trick

C announces that he must be wearing a white hat. He reasons as follows:

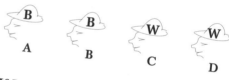

If I was wearing a black hat then D would see three black hats and know that he must be wearing a white hat (since all the hats are not the same color). Since D has not spoken, therefore he must see a white hat on my head.

Missouri?

Amazingly this can be solved all on one side of the river. Stand opposite some mark such as a bush on the other bank. Call that point X and the point where you are standing Y. Now walk perpendicularly to XY a measured distance—say 4 yards or meters—and mark this point with a branch. Call it A. Go on the same distance to mark another point B.

Now walk perpendicularly to YAB away from the river until you see the bush and the branch (points X and A) line up by line of sight. Call this point C. Then the width of the river is BC. This is because the two triangles XYA and ABC are identical.

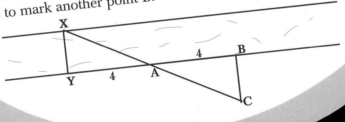

Eye Test

There are two possible ways it could be:

Passing Grade in Art

Place the paper on the side of a cylindrical bottle. Use the compasses as though to draw a circle and, on the curved surface, they will draw an ellipse.

10—UNCOMMON LATERALS

Three-peat!

a) First solution: 4—there are four letters in the word "four."
b) Second solution: 30—30 letters in "the correct answer to this question."
c) Third solution: 0—0 has 0 letters.

Postpaid

The man was a stamp collector and Elvis Presley fan. The U.S. Post Office brought out a special Elvis stamp, so the man sent it to a fictitious address. It was returned marked "Return to Sender," the title of one of Elvis's greatest hits.

Too Long!
He put it diagonally in a box 12 feet long and 5 feet wide.

InDEFinite
Understudy and overstuffed have RSTU in order.

Poker Face
Neither wins. A regular pack of cards does not have five aces.

Button Up
You put 3 buttons in the first cup, 3 buttons in the second cup and 3 buttons in the third cup. Then you put the third cup into the fourth cup. Every cup now has 3 buttons inside it.

Somehow
The word "wholesome".

How Irregular!
Fill the glass half full and then stir in salt to make the water denser. Add the raw egg which will float on top of the salty water. Then carefully add fresh

water. It will lie over the salty water and the egg will float in the middle.

Nonplussed

"One plus twelve" is an anagram of "two plus eleven".

Evening the Odds

Heads are more likely than tails but the chance of a heads then tails pair of tosses is equal to the chance of a tails then heads pair of tosses. Keep tossing the coin in pairs of tosses. One person backs heads/tails to come up first. The other person backs tails/heads to come up first.

Elbow Room

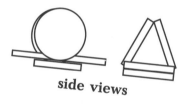

side views

Black Sheep?

Chuck's uncle is only 17 years old so he is not yet entitled to vote.

11—LOGIC PUZZLES

A-stounding!
101–One hundred and one.

Check This Out
WW __ BB
W __ WBB
WBW __ B
WBWB __
WB __ BW
__ BWBW
B __ WBW
BBW __ W
BB __ WW

(Now try WWW __ BBB.)

Cube It
No. Consider the central cube. It has six separate surfaces which must be made by six separate cuts.

Don't Tell
44. If her age minus 2 is divisible by 7 and 3 then that number must be a multiple of 21. This makes it easy to find her age.

Time Out
Yes. Imagine the holy man starting his climb up and his identical twin starting to

descend the mountain at the same time. There must be a point where the two of them cross.

Wrap Rap

Ten wrappers get you one bar of CHOCKOBLOCK. So it appears that one wrapper is worth 1/10th of a bar. But this 1/10th of a bar has 1/10th of a wrapper on it which is worth 1/100th of a bar, and so on indef-initely. If the wrapper is worth 1/10 +1/100 + 1/1000, etc., then this equates to 1/9th of a bar. Is the answer realistic? Yes. If you have 9 wrappers, go into a shop, ask for a bar and then take off its wrapper. Put it with the nine others to make 10 to pay for the bar!

Bad Bill

Many people get confused on this one. The person next door comes out even so the man's gain is the shopkeeper's loss. The man gains $20 in cash and the $30 boots. The shopkeeper loses $20 in cash and the $30 boots, making $50 in all.

Lethal Dose

Just before the start of the contest, the lateral-thinking alchemist took a draught of his own poison, which happened to be slow-acting enough. Then he poured away his poison and put water into the flask for his poison. When he drank his opponent's stronger poison he was saved. But when his opponent drank water and then his own strong poison, he had taken only one poison and died.

Duel à Trois

Con should point his gun in the air and deliberately miss. It's in his best interest that the two best shots shoot it out until only one is left. Then, on Con's turn he has a 50/50 chance of hitting his opponent. If he misses, his opponent could also miss, giving Con another 50/50 chance. This means that Con has the best chance overall of winning the contest and his chance is better than 50/50.

Hat Check

The first man can see 19 hats. He counts the number of black hats in front of him. If the number is odd he says "Black." If it is even he says "White." The second man can now work out the color of his hat based on the total number of black hats in front of him. For example, if he can see 7 black hats and he hears the first man say "White" he knows that his hat must be black to make an even number of black hats seen by the first man. The same process applies for all the other men in turn. In this way, they can guarantee to save 19 men. The first man has a 50/50 chance of being right so the expected result is 19.5 saved out of 20.

Early Pickup

They met at 7:20 p.m. In this puzzle, the distances and speeds are irrelevant. The important thing is that the car travels at a steady speed. It takes 20 minutes less time than it normally would. This must mean that the journey was shorter by 10 minutes each way, so they met 10 minutes earlier than usual.

Crossings

Let's call the four people 1, 2, 4, and 10, denoting how long it takes them each to cross. This is the best sequence:

1) 1 and 2 cross
2) 2 returns
3) 4 and 10 cross
4) 1 returns
5) 1 and 2 cross

The total elapsed time of the crossing is 17 minutes.

Clock on a String

You light both ends of one string and one end of the second tring. When the first string burns out exactly half an hour has passed. You immediately light the other end of the second string and hat will complete its burning in another 15 minutes, making 45 minutes in all.

Secret Numbers

The numbers are 5, 20, and 24. There are no two integers x,y such that $xy = 120$ and $x + y = 25$, so each number must either be part of the sum to 25 or part of the product of 120.

Let's look at the possible solutions:

a)

13, 12, 10
17, 15, 8
19, 6, 20
21, 4, 30
22, 3, 40
23, 2, 60
120, 1, 24

b)

15, 10, 12
15, 10, 8
20, 5, 6
20, 5, 24
24, 1, 5

None of the combinations in group a is the answer because the holder of the first number of the group would guess the answer immediately (e.g., if you have 13 as your number, you can guess the answer easily).

At the time of the second guess, all the people know the answer is one from group b. But after the second guess, they can figure out that:

The first combination of group b, 15 10 12, is not the answer (otherwise the holder of 12 would know it); the second combination of group b, 15 10 8, is not the answer either (otherwise the holder of 8 would know it). The same with the third and fourth combinations: 20 5 6 is not the answer (otherwise the holder of 6 would know it); and 24 1 5 is not the answer (otherwise the holder of 1 would know it).

Therefore, 20 5 24 is the only possible solution.

12—YET MORE WALLIES

1. You have two choices: the letter t (in alphab<u>et</u>), or the letter a in (th<u>e a</u>lphabet).

2. The pavement.

3. England always began with an E and end always began with an E.

4. The noise of the bike.

5. A hole.

6. A wedding ring.

7. Otto's car is a BMW.

8. Make mashed potatoes.

9. An armchair.

10. None—they were copycats!

11. Because seven ate nine!